CONTENTS

02 / TOY FACTORY

04 / DALMATIAN DOG MOTIF

06 / GRANDMA KNITTING SOCKS IN HER ARMCHAIR

08 / LIBRARY

10 / MAGICIAN

12 / THE GIRL IN THE GARDEN WATERING THE FLOWERS

14 / KIDS ON THE PLAYGROUND.

16 / PUPPIES AND KITTENS PLAYING TOGETHER

18 / HALLOWEEN COSTUMES FOR KIDS

20 / CHILDREN AND A BUNCH OF TOYS

22 / CUDDLING PETS

24 / THE CAT STOLE THE SAUSAGE

26 / BAROQUE GIRL SITTING ON A DRESSER

28 / APPLES AND SNAKES

Find 15 Hidden Objects In The Picture

Find 12 Hidden Objects In The Picture

05

Find 10 Hidden Objects In The Picture

07

Find 11 Hidden Objects In The Picture

FIND **OWL** IN THE PICTURE

Find 11 Hidden Objects In The Picture

FIND THE **RABBIT** IN THE PICTURE

Find 10 Hidden Objects In The Picture

13

Find 11 Hidden Objects In The Picture

FIND THE **TIGER** IN THE PICTURE

Find 10 Hidden Objects In The Picture

Find 11 Hidden Objects In The Picture

FIND CAT IN THE PICTURE

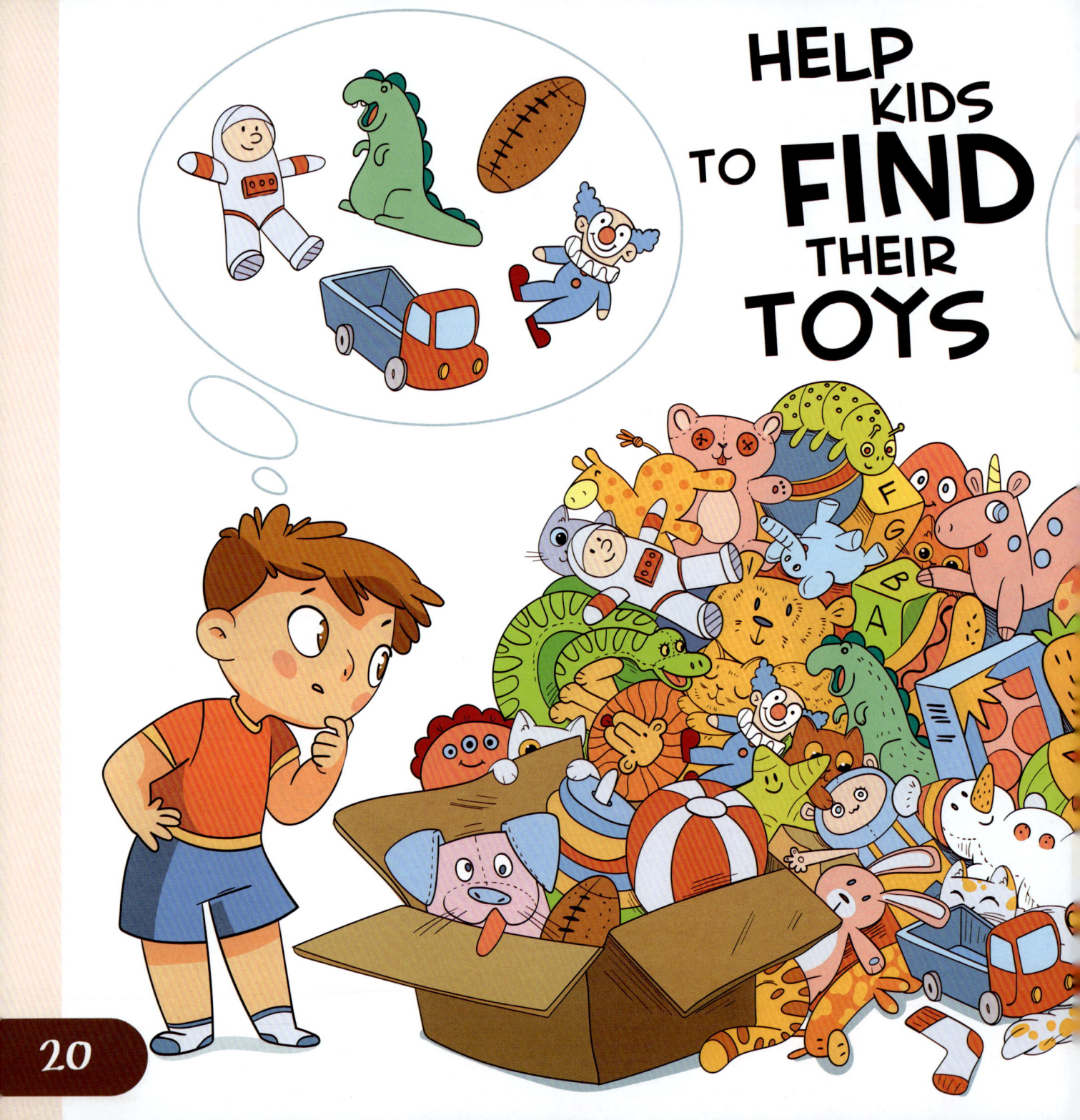

Find 11 Hidden Objects In The Picture

Find 11 Hidden Objects In The Picture

23

Find 10 Hidden Objects In The Picture

Find 10 Hidden Objects In The Picture

Find 10 Hidden Objects In The Picture

29

ANSWER

Page 2 Answers

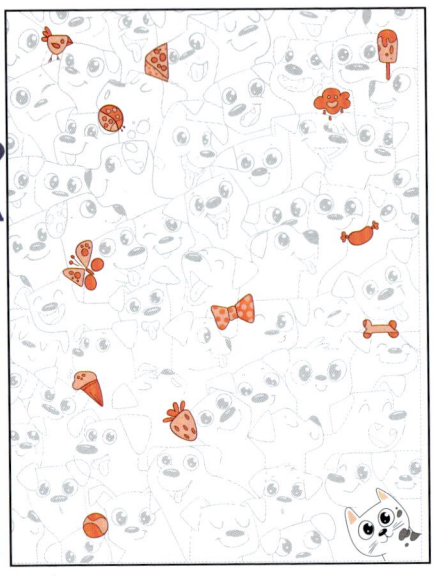
Page 4 Answers

Page 6 Answers

Page 16 Answers

Page 18 Answers

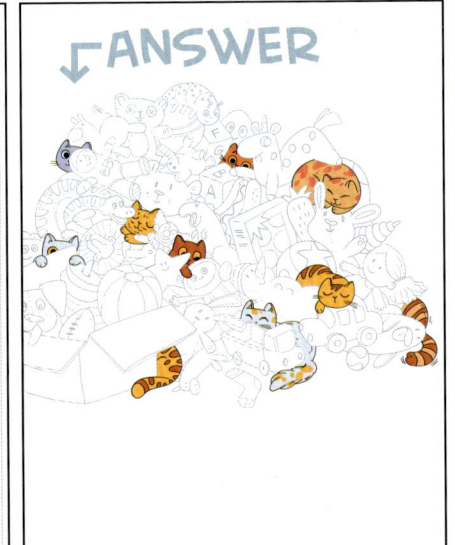
↳ANSWER

Page 20 Answers

Page 10 Answers

Page 12 Answers

Page 14 Answers

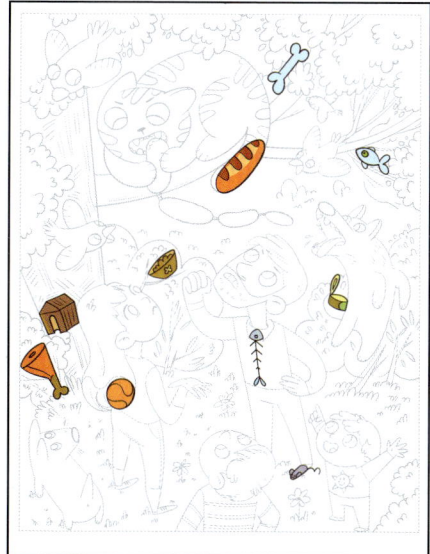

Page 24 Answers

Page 26 Answers

Page 28 Answers